21st Century
Basic Skills
Library

BABY ZOO ANIMALS
ELEPHANTS

by Josh Gregory

Cherry Lake Publishing • Ann Arbor, Michigan

3

Published in the United States of America
by Cherry Lake Publishing
Ann Arbor, Michigan
www.cherrylakepublishing.com

Content Adviser: Dr. Stephen S. Ditchkoff, Professor of Wildlife Sciences,
Auburn University, Auburn, Alabama

Photo Credits: Cover and page 1, ©Francois van Heerden/Shutterstock,
Inc.; page 4, ©Mark Eaton/Dreamstime.com; page 6, ©Duncan Noakes/
Dreamstime.com; page 8, ©Gail Johnson/Dreamstime.com; page 10,
©Zenpix/Dreamstime.com; page 12, ©Steve Wilson/Shutterstock,
Inc.; page 14, ©Michael Elliott/Dreamstime.com; page 16, ©SouWest
Photography/Shutterstock, Inc.; page 18, ©worradirek/Shutterstock, Inc.;
page 20, ©Anke van Wyk/Shutterstock, Inc.

Library of Congress Cataloging-in-Publication Data
Gregory, Josh.
Elephants / by Josh Gregory.
    p. cm. — (21st century basic skills library) (Baby zoo animals)
  Includes bibliographical references and index.
  ISBN 978-1-61080-452-3 (lib. bdg.) — ISBN 978-1-61080-539-1 (e-book) —
ISBN 978-1-61080-626-8 (pbk.)
1. Elephants—Infancy—Juvenile literature. 2. Zoo animals—Infancy—
Juvenile literature. 3. Captive elephants—Juvenile literature. I. Title.
  SF408.6.E44G74 2013
  599.67—dc23   2012001723

Cherry Lake Publishing would like to acknowledge
the work of The Partnership for 21st Century Skills.
Please visit www.21stcenturyskills.org for more information.

Printed in the United States of America
Corporate Graphics Inc.
July 2012
CLFA11

TABLE OF CONTENTS

Big Babies

Have you ever seen **elephants** at a zoo? They can be a lot of fun to watch.

You might see a baby elephant.

It is much smaller than the adult elephants. But it is still big!

Baby elephants are called **calves**. An elephant mother has one calf at a time.

A calf weighs more than most adult humans when it is born. A new calf is about 3 feet (1 meter) tall.

Calves have long tails and short **trunks**.

They can stand up just a few minutes after they are born.

They learn to walk about an hour later.

Life in the Zoo

You can see elephants at zoos around the world.

Baby elephants are very playful. **Zookeepers** let them play with toys.

Elephants love to swim and relax in pools.

You can see them spraying water from their trunks.

This helps them stay cool.

You might hear elephants use loud noises to call each other.

They can make close to 70 different sounds.

Elephants use sounds to show their feelings.

Calves drink milk from their mothers until they are about 2 years old.

They start eating plants when they are about 6 months old.

Growing Up

Calves grow and change as they get older.

They learn to grab and hold things with their trunks.

Their **tusks** also grow larger.

Elephants are adults when they are around 12 years old.

Then they can have babies of their own.

Soon there will be new baby elephants at the zoo!

Find Out More

BOOK

Clarke, Ginjer L. *Baby Elephant*. New York: Grosset & Dunlap, 2009.

WEB SITE

San Diego Zoo—Animal Bytes: Elephant
www.sandiegozoo.org/animalbytes/t-elephant.html
Read facts and check out pictures of elephants.

Glossary

calves (KAVZ) babies of certain animals, such as elephants

elephants (EL-uh-funts) large mammals with trunks that live in Africa and Asia

trunks (TRUNGKS) the long noses of elephants

tusks (TUHSKS) the long, curved, pointed teeth that stick out of the mouths of some animals, including elephants

zookeepers (ZOO-kee-purz) workers who take care of animals at zoos

Home and School Connection

Use this list of words from the book to help your child become a better reader. Word games and writing activities can help beginning readers reinforce literacy skills.

a	can	hear	minutes	short	time
about	change	helps	months	show	to
adult	cool	hold	more	smaller	toys
adults	close	hour	most	soon	trunks
after	different	humans	mother	sounds	tusks
also	drink	in	mothers	spraying	until
an	each	is	much	stand	up
and	eating	it	new	start	use
are	elephant	just	noises	stay	very
around	elephants	larger	of	still	walk
as	ever	later	old	swim	watch
at	feelings	learn	older	tails	water
babies	feet	let	one	tall	weighs
baby	few	life	other	than	when
be	from	long	own	the	will
big	fun	lot	plants	their	with
born	get	loud	play	them	world
but	grab	love	playful	then	years
calf	grow	make	pools	there	you
call	growing	meter	relax	they	zoo
called	has	might	see	things	zookeepers
calves	have	milk	seen	this	zoos

Fast Facts

Habitat: Grasslands and forests

Range: African elephants live throughout most of Africa. Asian elephants are found in India, Nepal, and throughout Southeast Asia

Average Height: Between 8 and 11 feet (2.4 and 3.4 meters)

Average Weight: Males usually weigh between 11,000 and 15,000 pounds (4,990 and 6,800 kilograms). Females usually weigh between 6,000 and 8,000 pounds (2,720 and 3,600 kg).

Life Span: About 50 to 65 years

Index

About the Author

Josh Gregory writes and edits books for children. He lives in Chicago, Illinois.